Responses to *I Have Decided To Remain Vertical*:

Gayelene has a distinctive voice – her poems are by turns hilarious, sorrowful and beautiful. They are unflinchingly precise while retaining their affectionate core. Her perfect balance of humour and pathos really hit me – I loved every page.

Ann Shenfield

Gayelene Carbis's poems in *I Have Decided To Remain Vertical* capture the catastrophe and beauty of daily living, the ache and triumph. These are poems which are vulnerable yet unflinching; complex, corporeal, intimate; rich, well-observed, funny and precise. There is a rare emotional acuity in Gayelene's work, of tenderness, and anger, and power. Her poems speak to each other and beyond, reverberating long after being read.

Katia Ariel,
author of *The Swift Dark Tide* (memoir)

Gayelene Carbis writes into memory and place with such candour and clarity. The work radiates from the particularities of a childhood, a body and then flows out to a largeness, an epic kind of vision and compassion. The pain and love of family is rendered without sentimentality. Observations of daily life, here and elsewhere, are deceptively simple, conversational at times. But they are carved, wrought with finesse and an eye for how words work on the page, and in our mind's ear, each poem its own song. Often they are like tiny documentaries, a window into work, art, others, the world. This is poetry that shifts its lens effortlessly, a meditation on how a writer, an artist is formed. Gayelene's words move us out into the world and carry us back to ourselves.

Emilie Collyer

For those of us interested in the inner dialogue of a person who lives a complicated but rich life this book is for you. Human relationships in all form and guises are depicted throughout this collection, illuminated by Carbis's succinct, incisive, wry depictions of dialogue, perceptions and emotions. The writing has a translucent quality that lifts the retelling of sad, bad or mad experiences from heartrending, to charming, wry observations of human nature. Throughout, there is a sense that where before there had been confusion and loss, there is now evidence of learning about life; acceptance of how this life has come packaged. Warmth of understanding of others permeates these writings, the experience is uplifting; immersing.

Ann Locanini

Raw and honest, piercing and revelatory, this beautiful collection *I Have Decided To Remain Vertical* is a personal confrontation with the past and an encounter with the present. Each poem is a gem telling a story of loss, love and longing. With courage and unflinching self-examination, Gayelene Carbis has created a tapestry of those moments in time that make up a life.

Marcia Jacobs

Previous collection, *Anecdotal Evidence*:

[A] particularly personal, indeed intimate book, by turns playful, poignant, hilarious, nostalgic, brisk, effusive, wry, fragile, intricate, sexy, ironic, scathing, loving – and occasionally all of these at once ... propelled by a lively intelligence and a distinctive, sometimes barbed wit, but allied with a discipline of craft and a toughness of psychological insight that can be easily missed while we enjoy the ride ... There is complexity and ambiguity, and both joy and pain ... alongside a compelling and compelled exhilaration in the recounting.

Alex Skovron
(excerpt from Launch speech)

I Have Decided To
Remain Vertical

'St Kilda Morning: Souvenir of Luxor,' oil on canvas, by Anselm van Rood.

www.awakeningtheeye.net

I Have Decided To Remain Vertical

Gayelene Carbis

PUNCHER & WATTMANN

First published in 2022
Published by Puncher and Wattmann
PO Box 279
Waratah NSW 2298

https://www.puncherandwattmann.com
web@puncherandwattmann.com

ISBN   9781922571489

Cover image: detail from 'St Kilda Morning: Souvenir of Luxor,' oil on canvas,
          by Anselm van Rood. www.awakeningtheeye.net
Cover design by Libby Austen
Typesetting by Morgan Arnett
Printed by Lightning Source International

NATIONAL
LIBRARY
OF AUSTRALIA

A catalogue record for this
work is available from the
National Library of Australia

Contents

Marrying Freud

Marrying Freud: Ladder to the Moon	13
Dictionary of Beautiful Words	15
The Lovely Place	16
The Good Breast	17
Errand	18
Our House	20
Repeats	22
Love Like This	24
The Price We Pay	25
Laundry	27
At a Bus Station in Calgary	29
A Woman from Carnegie	30
The Baker's Daughter	31
Hedda Gabler	32
Postcard from Paris	33
No Room at the Inn	35
Notice to Vacate	37
My Lover's in Business and Out Most Nights	39
Ribbons	40
After Sylvia	41

Red Horse by the River

St Kilda Morning	45
Snake	48
Not Marrying the Egyptian	50
The Dead Sea	52
Family	53

Christmas at 11am in Launceston   54

'Don't Break the Bunny'   56

You Are Not / Your Poetry   57

Egyptians   58

Haunted   61

Red Horse by the River   64

The Object of The Father All at Sea   65

Lessons on Life from My Sister in First Year   68

Girl in Front   69

In the best of all possible worlds   70

Morsels   71

Your Mind on the Dead   72

Writing Companion   74

Laura's Pergolas   75

The Bride Who Became Frightened When She Saw Life Opened

The Bride Who Became Frightened When She Saw Life Opened   81

The Call   82

Annotated Memories   84

The Photograph Travels With Us Through Time   86

The Day You Left   88

Not Sending You Poetry   91

Daddy Long Legs   94

Layers   95

Januaries   96

Horses   97

Embodiment in Quill   99

After 'Still Life with Babette's Jug #2'   100

The Memory of Colour   102

Acknowledgements   103

In memory of
Judith Rodriguez
and
Ania Walwicz

This book is also dedicated to
my father, my mother, and my brother,
with much love

Marrying Freud

Marrying Freud: Ladder to the Moon

After 'Ladder to the Moon,' a painting by Georgia O'Keefe
I.M. Ania Walwicz

I dreamt I married Freud.

He was turning down the bed when I turned to see him,
one hand held midair as if he were conducting
something, an alertness on his face at a faint strain
of music, or a sound outside.

I thought of strutting past him in my new sleekness, all those
kilos I'd lost without him, while he was away and I was
alone. I'm so small after all, and those seventy kilos
had surrounded me, like I was keeping the world away.

Then he went away and now they've gone. So here I am,
standing at the door watching him as he prepares
in that painstaking way he has, slow but steady, and I thought –
I'm really not sure about this.

I'd leapt into love and sex (not in that order, he'd say)
when I was young and green, I didn't know what I wanted –
a man, a house, a baby, a life. I knew I needed to write,
nothing else could have me.

I would never see a man now, I don't know how other women
do it. Justifying male therapists with father issues and transference.
Power is always between you, like the sheets,
like sex, as he'd say. When Freud patted the sheet

as if it was his dog, I was galvanised into
action. I went back to the kitchen, sat at the table and wrote
about my day. It took me all night. He hates
sleeping alone. I stayed in the kitchen and when he came out,
bleary-eyed in the morning, I let him make his own coffee,
I'm not his fucking mother. When I woke from the dream, I decided –

there are going to be a few changes around here.

Dictionary of Beautiful Words

for L

I am learning a new word every day and have even more sympathy for
my students and friends learning English as an Additional Language.
*Unless you're regularly using them, you say, of course it's hard.
It's almost impossible when they're not beautiful words:
isopolity, epigone, contextomy — we don't go around
saying these things. You need to keep in your mind
a dictionary of beautiful words. Like lovely places
you can always return to.*

The Lovely Place

The owner demolished the front garden.
Camellias were removed. The trees
were cut down. To make way for
a concrete driveway. I drive past
mourning the house where we once
lived. How it's been irrevocably
changed. I, too, am irrevocable.
We can never return to a place
that's not there anymore.

The Good Breast

It was Christmas Eve at St Vincent's Hospital breakfast time when they
brought me round it was morning and just before nine a bell in the
background rang in my mother's sleep and she almost believed she'd
been dreaming of convents but it was only a memory of primary school
and climbing the rope to ring out lunchtime she says she offered but I
turned away I baulked at my mother's breast wouldn't take to the nipple
there are babies like that (my brother too) spitting out mother's milk
I was swaddled in and brought to her bed but she worn out from birth
waved me away terrified she'd drop me and like an egg I'd crack shells
on the floor or she'd sleep and roll on top of me with her milk-laden
breasts maybe they brought me for feeding yes it's hard to get a story
straight when someone says why do you want to know as if you are
interrogating a war crime maybe I knew that food was dangerous
there were few nutrients there or it could be it came from her young
green ignorant scared brown from the sun yellow it's supposed to come
naturally but does it a girl unschooled alone in a bed but still love
is not pure that has no boundaries my mother's milk must have dried
up and withered away and died but she never cried no use crying
over spilt milk she'd say and she took me home and loved me to death

Errand

again she hit me over the head with the wrong rice

the plastic container thwacked hard as if
its sides might split and bamboo shoots spring
out, like snakes from a Medusa's head

the peas jumped around, giant marbles
juggled in a trembling hand trying to beat
a school champion or the kid next door

in her kitchen
with its paint peeling
and bits and pieces of plaster

falling down around us
(and my father a solid plasterer,
a builder who never built us a house)

my tears silently fell on the cold lino
it was as if I could feel that coldness
in my frozen feet

all those days and nights of knocking
on Dad's head
raps ringing out as if it was wood

are you all there?
she could never get through, she said
there was nobody there

my cousin Kathy laughed out loud
at things that never happened
in her house

I kissed Kathy hard
when she went home
and made sure it hurt

Our House

Our house was filled with violence and parties. My friends were always welcome. My mother always bought me birthday cakes from Paterson's. My mother treated me like a movie star most of the time and at other times she called me a cunt. She hit me over the head with a container of rice when I brought the wrong rice home. She told me to leave school and get a job at Safeway when I was fifteen but said nothing about Safeway when I left school and went on the dole so then I knew it wasn't really about Safeway. My mother was volatile. I asked my father once how he saw my childhood (had no idea what he'd say) and he said it was violent. I left school and stayed home. I became a party girl. I went out with lots of boys. And men. My mother treated me like a movie star and said I was special. My mother made out like all the men were in love with me. My mother said I was hopeless. I could barely tie my own shoes. I wasn't allowed to touch the washing machine. Even the toaster was a vexation to my mother's spirit. Because of the crumbs. My mother lived in the kitchen. I sang and danced in the lounge room. I sang and danced in my bedroom. I stayed in my bedroom. A room of one's own isn't enough. I stayed home when they went on drives on Sunday. My mother hated me biting my nails. I hated her. She was the love of my life. No she wasn't. Judy, Julie, Barbra. I was three. Seven. Thirteen. 'Over The Rainbow.' *The Sound of Music.* Streisand in *A Star is Born*. My mother was critical. My mother bought cakes. And crumpets. My mother gave me lemonade and dark peppermint chocolate when I was sick. We fought like furies when I turned thirteen. Fourteen, fifteen, sixteen. Seventeen. I dropped out of school, I didn't know why. I thought I feared failure, or success. They seemed the same thing. My mother didn't say anything. My mother stopped telling me to get a job at Safeway and I just stayed home. I stayed in my room and sang and danced around and started going to parties and clubs and went out with boys and men and wanted to be a movie star. But then I kept going back to school. I tried three times. To return. To finish. But somehow I couldn't. I kept dropping out. No one noticed. Or if they did they said nothing. I remember every day I headed off to uni as a mature-age student, I couldn't breathe till I turned right at the end of our street and walked further away from our house in the street where we lived. Where my mother was.

Repeats

My brother brings her a birthday present.
Always too early or too late.
He never remembers the date,
even though it always follows
Father's Day. He forgets that too.
He can't wait. He comes into the kitchen
carrying the blue-ray in a box
in a big yellow bag. 'Here! Happy Birthday!'
My mother reacts the way I've seen
so many times before. My brother reacts to
her reaction. I sit there trying not to react
to either of them. She doesn't smile. She sniffs.
She looks at me sitting there not looking at her
or him. She is always after a collusion.
I look at my dinner. There is far too much
on my plate. Here we go. The dialogue
stuck like a record in a groove.
I sit there and say nothing, watching them
the way I watch television,
leaving noise on in the background.
My brother looks at me too, looking for
our old alliance. I refuse both of them.
We move on to blue-ray. He's fed up
with the DVD. He says it's from
the two of us. 'You didn't buy that for me,
you bought it for yourself.' 'No no, you needed it.
You'll love it.' And round and round we go.
He explains how it all works, the world;
DVD's are on the way out. Her world is shrinking,
growing obsolete. Her leg aches with arthritis.

Her hip hurts. Nothing was ever good enough
anyway. She only ever wanted Boronia.
Decades of Boronia, perfume or powder,
soap, that's all you could buy her.
I come back to Father's Day.
'Shall we take him out?' I say.
'What – kill him?' my brother says.
My brother has a hammer
he wants to take to her DVD player,
it's been playing up, 'There'd be so much satisfaction
in smashing that thing to smithereens,' he says.
'Blow it up. Blast it out of here.'
'How long have you been at the bakery now?'
I ask him but what I really mean is:
How long have you been living here
and when are you going to *go?*
It's all set up before we get to our tea.
My brother raves about the blue-ray
waiting for us in the lounge room.
'Come on!' he calls. 'Come and watch something!'
But I've seen enough. I'm going home.

Love Like This

Before my father got fat he used to say he was
trim taut and terrific. And he was. Movie-star looks,
an athletic build. He'd swim sixty laps at the Prahran Pool,
up and down with my baby brother on his back. A chunky
little body and a head of golden curls in the sky. Those
chubby hands holding him. Never falling off and never
letting go as my father pressed on stroke after stroke. And we
were so beautiful then, all of us. Now we are older, my father old.
But my brother, my brother has been a boy in a grown man's body
forever. Last year he turned forty. None of us was allowed near
him. He turned forty alone. My father told me my brother had said
he had nothing to show for it. When my brother talked to me
for the first time in ten years, I couldn't concentrate on
what he was saying. All I could see was that boy
on his father's back, waiting for the sun
to come out and shine on him.

The Price We Pay

I keep men waiting
as my father before me
kept us waiting.
my brother and I were always
standing by the sidewalk
on tenterhooks, our need
like a big red tongue
hanging out and panting
for a drop of rain
in drought.
bills were never paid in our house.
our landlord (a nice man)
waited months
before he told my mother
the rent hadn't been paid.
we spent a whole childhood
outside houses
fighting in our father's car
while women served our father
(such a nice man)
coffee and cake.
the day was drawn out
as a watched kettle.
we were boiling.
we wanted our lives
to take off, like a train
with a clear destination.
instead, we rearranged things
round our father,
believing every time

he'd turn up
but finding ourselves
always alone on a platform
watching trains pull out
without us.
now I call myself feminist
and make the men I live with
pay.
it's taken a lifetime to learn
my father's promises are full
of air and leave us steaming.
and yet he's so well-meaning.
yes he's a man who means well,
he tells us all
'leave it with me.'
we spend the rest of our lives
trying not to.

Laundry

My father has laundry to do on Sunday.
Which means he can come to Carnegie.
Which means he can see me.

My father lives three suburbs
five kilometres
five minutes
away from Carnegie.

I see him when he can get away.
I don't go there because that is their home.
He wouldn't mind but his wife would.

It's convenient to kill two birds with one stone.
I am a bird, he is a stone.
Sometimes I could kill my father.

We will go to the laundry and finish coffee in time
for the clothes to finish the wash cycle.
This is called catching up with my father.

He would say you don't do this —
you just don't do that —
talk about your dirty laundry in public.

Yet he takes my poetry and plays,
my stories, pretty well.
I apologise after poems, after plays.

But he says, *Well, why not?*
It's the truth. He can take it—
in the films he sees, the books he reads.

But catching up for coffee is conversation
light and frothy as foam.
If you bring up anything difficult,

anything he finds depressing,
he looks like you've dragged him down,
or you've put him through the wringer.

And who wants to have that effect
on their father? Over coffee, he keeps
looking at his watch.

He keeps track of the time, so he's not late
for the laundry. We finish when he's finished
and head back for the dryers.

I spend the rest of the day
trying not to cry, trying
to write this poem.

At a Bus Station in Calgary

When I was young and empty *
I did not know I was under-fed

I thought my mother filled me with food
and her sustenance gave me life:

They poured Christ into my mind
and I became a vessel

so full, I could not think
or feel:

I took in everything around me
like bread soaked in vinegar, or wine

I did not know the blood of Christ was bitter,
that wrung through,

I'd be dry.

after a line from a poem by Galway Kinnell, 'The Still Time'

A Woman from Carnegie

I used to see her on the tram or train, her jeep brimming with books; plastic bags tied to the side flapping in the wind, noisy little sounds that caught your ear and made you turn your head. The bag lady threw Shakespeare into her monologues; knew Wordsworth and Keats and Byron; pieces of poetry; and there she was pushing her jeep at a Streisand concert, her white hair wild, her big blue raincoat wide open, a misshapen dress tent-like and loose round her stomach, her face flushed from weather and walking. She walked miles. I used to follow her. I tried to ask where she went to school, where she lived, where she'd grown up, but nothing I could say could contain her. She was garrulous; a gruff manner, a rough voice; and anything in her mind might come out of her mouth. There's no room now on trams or trains for jeeps and I haven't seen bag ladies in ages. But you do wonder where they've all gone; why I was so filled with fascination, and fear. I had a best friend at uni who used to say if she ever wrote a thesis, a Masters, a PhD, she'd do it on bag ladies. Kate Grenville's Lillian had haunted her. I never thought to ask her why. Yet I understood it too, at another level. Another friend, also from uni, told me no matter what, she'd never leave her husband. She'd had, she said, a mad mother and an absent father, who was an actor. She'd known poverty as a child and she was never going back there. She could still remember being seven years old and doing the shopping. Lying awake at night thinking about money. She was forty years old and still afraid of ending up a bag lady. There used to be bag ladies and mad women on the tram and I'd be there in my short skirts and stilettos and I'd look at them and they'd look at me and for some reason I incensed them. My sandals and my lipstick. I'd always smile, as if to say I was benevolent, but they'd snarl at me and start screaming obscenities and I'd feel like erupting into this insane laughter and it was so hard to stop. I'd be forced to move and I was always frightened but trying not to show it. I can still see the bag lady in her big blue raincoat, pushing that jeep round Colonial Stadium where Streisand was. I haven't seen her for a very long time in this suburb, but I still think about all the things we share.

The Baker's Daughter

After Ophelia's soliloquy from 'Hamlet'

I flow downstream, north-mad, beneath
the netherworld of dreams: not air, but sea
and stream and creek: a kind of death wrought
from the kin of love: in theatres world over,
your iambic flourishes cast me strew: impresario
and scholar, you make literal the shadows:
too mindful, we die to our truer selves, calling father!
But the fathers, all air, walk as ghosts over the grave ground.

Hedda Gabler

she burns his manuscript and I cry out –

see the flames rising up like flags
of protest, the smoke stifling the air
and seeping into her black lonely lung
which waits for the wound. What lengths
will she go to? How could she – ?

Yet there you are, 3am at some incinerator
in an industrial backwoods, shoving down
a chute twenty years of your life to make
space for me in our new life.

All those proofs which could be shored up as
evidences of who you were and where
you've been have gone up in smoke or
lie buried under trash-mounds.

And you insist I know you now
two years down the track but all I can think about is
all that work you're throwing away –
old poetry and songs you wrote for other lovers.

You leave me here at Santucci's cafe
looking through a window waiting while
you go back home to organise the furniture
so we can begin our lives.

Postcard from Paris

I stood by the Seine and I could swear I called you,
as if a river holds telephones with wires running like waves.

~

I followed your footsteps, found Shakespeare and Co,
remembered you'd said we'd go to Paris together, someday.

~

You said you'd left a book of your own poetry, they had
placed it on one of the bookshelves and you kept returning
to find it, half-hoping it hadn't been sold.

~

I looked for your poetry but if it was ever here,
it had gone now; the way memory moves in and out
of consciousness, the way Paris will always be
the place where I was trying to reach you
while you were back home with *her*,
sending half-truths and stories down the line,
sending me emails on separation anxiety,
as if stories and papers justified your betrayal.

~

You'd told me about writers in Paris, Beckett
and Joyce in the bookshop. Went out and bought me
A Moveable Feast. Yet you weren't here.

~

Once in the flat, not long before I left, we watched
The Last Time I Saw Paris and a friend asked us
'What were you both doing home in the middle
of the day?' That's gone too, but I remember
Elizabeth Taylor and how she always loved and
lost and how I could never understand how it was
possible to be so beautiful and still men could leave you.

~

When I called you from Paris from those phone booths
in the streets, you'd stopped saying 'Hello, beautiful'
when you heard my voice and you sounded strange.
I wanted to get a flight straight home
but the friends I was with stopped me.

~

Whatever was going to happen had already happened.

~

I bought a book from Shakespeare and Co
but forgot to tell you about it and by then
it was already too late.

~

I left that city but I am still
standing there by the Seine, my tears falling into
the thousands. They have run for centuries there.

No Room at the Inn

I needed to find someone to live with when you left.
I was desperate. And I needed a new doorbell and
my father went out and bought one, because I asked him to.
It worked for two days then stopped. It was worth ten dollars.

My father came to the door a few days later and rang the bell
but when it didn't work, he went and sat in his car and called me
from his mobile. I watched him from my window.
When I asked, he pretended he'd never been near the bell,

didn't know it didn't work. I told him I'd seen him. Walking up
to the door, pressing the button, then returning to his car.
Calling me on his mobile. I asked why he'd lied. He said
because I'd go on about it and he couldn't be bothered.

He has his own home (well, it's not his, it's *hers*). He doesn't
seem to comprehend how it feels to not have a home.
To have to live with a housemate. To have *you* leave.
There are people who will judge you and your house

by a broken doorbell, a lawn unmown, dishes left in the sink.
You never know what's important to somebody else.
I never know what's important to my father. Except of course
movies and books. And going out. And cakes. And chocolate.

Milk shakes. Driving around. Eating out. Restaurants. Getaways.
Travel. Cruises. Cafes. Chadstone. His wife. His house.
And the rule book he and his wife live by and seem to think
everyone else has read. I said to my father, *Someone could come,*

I wouldn't know they were there, I can't hear from upstairs if they knock.
Another time I asked my father if I could bring someone to
my (half-)sister's birthday. He said there wouldn't be enough room
at the table. He wouldn't have known if the someone was my partner,

my boyfriend, my lover – the man in the moon. How could he,
he hadn't seen me for more than five minutes or asked me
anything about my life in a year so how would he know who
I was with. If I was married or officially with someone for

six months, or six weeks (ok, let's not be ridiculous here,
I wasn't going to say six *days*), I guess that would make me
legitimate. And there might be – there just might be –
enough room at the table.

Notice to Vacate

The doctor tells my mother she has cancer but my mother tells him
she can't have surgery or start treatment because she needs to find

somewhere to live. By September. So it's soon. The doctor tells her,
I'm afraid you can't put cancer on hold. But my mother — who has

finally taken in my message that her situation with housing is serious —
there's no public housing, no community or social housing waiting

for her — even the homeless can't find a home — my mother tells
the doctor, *No, my daughter said I have to put this first. I need to find*

somewhere to live, she says. I'm not there but I can see the doctor
looking at her as if she's a child. I can see her innocence as she sits

there. And though she seems to think I can just walk in and take
control — talk to people, move around in the world and make things

happen — I can't wave a magic wand and make the developers disappear.
I can't give her back forty-three years of her life in her house. And then

there's the painful process of applying for public housing. 20-year waiting list.
And though I could rip up the piece of paper from the Department of

Human Services and Housing Authority that said 'Although you have
received a Notice to Vacate, your housing is deemed to be secure at this time,'

what would be the point? I ask if she cried when the doctor told her and
she said, *About what?* and I said, *About … having cancer.*

I was about to, she says, *but then I thought – what's the point? If you're going to snuff it, you're going to snuff it. No use crying about it.*

The doctor tells me, *She seems to think she has to find somewhere to live and that's more important – as if that's the most important thing here.*

It surprises me she tells strangers her private business, as if she's beyond it. He tries to talk to her (surgery, chemotherapy) but she just looks back at him

and says, *My daughter said* ...The doctor tells me over the telephone the things my mother said, he keeps repeating them. As if I can step in and save her.

My Lover's in Business and Out Most Nights

my friends say he's a phantom. i've made him up. he doesn't exist.
they look for signs and find none. i take up every space.
paraphernalia spreads itself around this house like smoke
that creeps under doors and sends him running into
the street for air. my ex says *if i lived with you, i wouldn't be*
coming home midnight or ten or eleven — i'd be with you.
do you ever see him? he says hoping but already shaking
his head *oh no, i'd be here with you* he says with such devotion
i think he forgets those nights he pushed me out the door took
my keys my money my clothes and me running to my mother or
neighbour knowing they'd be home, they're in most nights. 6am,
7, the lover's out the door. days, nights pass where i don't see him.
we miss each other mornings. he's gone by the time i'm up.
my light's switched off and so am i by the time he's back.
i hear his key in the door and lie there wondering where he's been.
i leave post-it-notes in the kitchen, and send letters, emails and he's
surprised, sounds shocked, *you write me emails every day!* i get
incredulity at the notes, my voice goes high as i cry *well you're*
never here! another time i ask if he can tell me when he might be
in or out. he says he's not checking into a hotel but i say isn't
that how you *live.* like this house is not a home but a *hotel?*
we are strangers sharing this place. sometimes a bed. a shoulder.
our bodies. if i'd known he lived like this i wouldn't be living
like this. no one told me living with a lover could be so lonely.

Ribbons

How nervously now a cold comes. I fear chaos. I know the wind carries more
than pollen. I know how felled a body can be by something that once seemed

so small. And yet we forget too, forget sweating in our beds, our heads heavy,
our legs shooting with pain. We have been here before. But twenty, thirty, forty

are nowhere near fifty. We stand on the other side looking back, saying —
Oh my God! I never knew I had such a tiny waist! Once I ran round an oval

in a picture-hat and my ribbons ran after me. They could never catch me,
nobody could. Now I have caught up with myself and I never wear ribbons.

There is a writer friend about my age who wears a red hibiscus in her hair,
on one side, as if she's in Hawaii. Another woman, from choir, wears red

ribbons and a red dress after Kate and Kathy calling out to Heathcliff. Ribbons
are still possible. And so is red. I am not dead after all, just half-alive after

asthma, the flu. Meanwhile I see those other women in my mind with their
flowers and their ribbons, and remember.

After Sylvia

'I don't expect you to write like
Sylvia Plath,' he said this morning.

This is how a day can break, with
needs tilting at your windmills.

The oil in your hair reeks of coconut.
Ink spills across paths you haven't taken.

'Sylvia was sad,' he said. 'She never
had the chance to confront, to resolve

her anger against her father's remoteness.
Sadness became madness.

She was more damaged than you are.
But be like Sylvia. Go back to your poem.

Face it. Call your father on his bullshit.
Your own rage. Don't explain.

Don't editorialise. Just say it. Read Sylvia.
Her poems. For their surgical precision.'

He adds: 'You need to take up that scalpel.'
I put down the phone thinking of

Birthday Letters, which he gave me
for my birthday, and return to my desk.

I hold my pen — like a knife.

Red Horse by the River

St Kilda Morning

After 'St Kilda Morning: Souvenir of Luxor,' oil on canvas, by Anselm van Rood

As soon as I see your *St Kilda Morning* – straightaway – I'm in Luxor

the perfect blue of the sky

      the palm trees

           the shape of the sea, the curve of the road

even the tram tracks are soft and pink and yellow like sand

      like the desert

there's something tropical – hot and humid

          that heat, that summer

that time I met Tarek

      which means Prince

         the Egyptian who took me to Egypt

the whirlwind romance – him here in Melbourne, and meeting me

and taking me home to meet his parents in Cairo

and then that trip down the Nile to the Valley of the Kings

and me on a boat watching the Nubian rowing us –

the sweat pouring off his skin

and Tarek telling me not to worry about him, he's used to it

the heat, the rowing, the sun on his skin

as if Tarek thought I thought the Nubian was being treated like

some kind of servant

I have been in thrall to all of my stories –

I made Tarek and Egypt into a story

I turned Luxor, turned my life, into material

and when I saw your *St Kilda Morning* I stepped right into it

as if I could make it into something else, be somewhere else

and now I discover

you too have travelled to Egypt, looking for that same light

but your eyes were always open and alive to the light

to your art

as my eyes have now opened, and are alive to the light

to my art

Snake

Last night
a huge python
slithered into
your mind.

The python
crawled
across unwashed clothes
in your mother's washing basket.

You told yourself:
what she
doesn't see
won't hurt her.

But poison
spilled
from
its mouth.

It left a trail
on your skin
that stung you
from sleep.

Then you woke
to find me
like Eve
at your rib.

You hold me close
and sometimes
even
tell me your dreams.

But when we
make love,
you withdraw
just before you come.

Afterwards,
I feel bereft.
Trails
on my skin.

Not Marrying the Egyptian

he tells me what they say and I call this intimacy

'Is it just sexual?' his mother asks him. 'Why aren't you married?' his brother asks. 'Why won't you marry her?' his mother says. 'Why won't you marry her?' echoes his brother.

'I'm going away ... on a holiday,' he says. 'Alone?' asks his mother. 'No.' 'With a friend ...?' 'Yes.' 'With her?' 'Yes.' 'But you told me it was over,' his mother says. 'What are you doing with her? What are you doing with your life?'

'What are you doing with your life?' his brother says. His mother cries when he tells her he's moving in with me. 'This is not how I brought you up,' she says. His mother cries more when she realizes we're sleeping together.

'This is not how I brought you up,' she cries. 'Why aren't you married yet? Why are you with him?' his brother asks me. 'You should get out,' his brother tells me. 'He might take you to Eden but he will never take you to Egypt.'

He says it's his family. His uncles, his cousins. His aunts. He can't explain *living together* to them. He can't explain sex. He has to fix his relationship with God. His solution is to abstain from sex.

The next time, he takes me. I am in Egypt with the Egyptian. The first thing he does is make a move on me as soon as we arrive at the apartment. He says he's sorry but I'm not sure who he's saying sorry to. It could be his God; it could be his mother.

'Do you see yourself as Egyptian or Australian, or both?' I ask. There's this long silence. Then he says, 'It's not a fair question.' I ask if he could be with someone from a different culture and he says it's more about religion than culture. 'What do you mean?' I say.

'I couldn't be with a Jew or a Muslim (though some of them are gorgeous) because when it comes to having children, we don't share fundamental beliefs,' he says. 'But you say you don't want children!' I say.

He doesn't answer. 'So what are you doing with *me* then?'

I've never wanted them. I'll never have them. He doesn't answer. 'Why aren't you with an Egyptian girl ...' I say. 'Why don't you *choose* to be with an Egyptian?' I say. 'It'd be easier.' 'You can't just go out with a girl, an Egyptian,' he says.

'Egyptian girls!' he says. 'I'd have to marry the fuckers,' he says. He says it's a joke. I'm not laughing. I am reeling from language.

He says *going out with* means marriage. There is no other way. It's his culture, his religion. His family.

'Why are you with me?' I say. 'You're not really with me.' 'I'm still here, aren't I?' he says.

The Dead Sea

We went to the Dead Sea but I didn't bring
my bathers so I couldn't go in. I had to
watch on the shore, I didn't know then
I'd never be back. I was young.
I thought rivers and seas and skies lasted
forever. I thought they'd wait for me.
I thought I could build bridges
back to anything, anywhere. Anyone.
I remember my Egyptian fiance's mother
had a checkered cloth on the table.
It reminded me of my mother's, back home
in Melbourne. But here, we were
eating pigeon, it had been roasted.
My mother's roasts were chicken or lamb
or pork and she always saved me
the crackling. Here we were in Hurghada,
we were in Cairo, we went to Alexandria.
My mother stayed home. My mother never
went anywhere. She's still never been on
a plane. My mother's life fills me with sadness.
I thought I had time to fill it with things –
Europe, or an island, somewhere, anywhere.
I didn't know, I didn't know, what life
had in store for us.

Family

We were so sad, we left our houses to live in a tree.
Of course we were together, our limbs tangled,
our breaths breathing in each other's bodies.
The tree told us we were temporary guests.
At night, we heard all the trees talking,
though we couldn't make out the words.
Murmurs seeped into our sleep and became
malignant in our dreams. In the mornings
we woke and saw we'd made something
monstrous out of fear. Our sanctuary
wouldn't save us. We swept our tears into
the streets, hid in the bark of our brooms
as if wood had become new skin.

Christmas at 11am in Launceston

The only time left. We turn up late. Unusual for us.
Door's locked. Dark inside. Bars on windows.
The Jailhouse Grill like a deserted prison.
I wonder how you'll react if they've got it
wrong. You don't take human failing well.
The world not working out as it should.
I hold my breath, waiting for the world
to give us its reckoning.

Back home, my mother will
put on the roast for my brother and the boys.
My brother's friends, men – but she calls them boys.
Friends without family. My father and his family
will be making their way to the other side
of the city where the rest of his family live.
I notice I say *his* when I mean *our*.
The sides were always separate. There was
always her side, which dominated, and his side,
and I always felt I had to choose.
I went with what felt comfortable.
I've always clung to comfort zones.

And maybe all this is why I'm here.
With you again, at Christmas.
Standing there in the street. Our fractured families.
Lovers we've had. All the broken relationships
we've had and still have now. Somewhere there,
a litany behind us. The two of us
turning to each other. Familiar as family.
We're like an old married couple, everyone says.

Looking for a little company. Friendship. Love.
Not wanting to be alone.

Suddenly we see someone. She heads for
the door. Opens it. And lets us in.

'Don't Break the Bunny'

Seventeen years of
enormous eggs (the largest you can find at Safeway)
and bunnies in beds, on pillows, outside my door and popping up
in unexpected places, you like a Big Easter Bunny and a Magician,
hiding birthday and Easter and Christmas presents in your car and closets
and under your bed, as if I was a child, or a lover or a life-mate –
someone you loved, at least – and I have been and you have been
all of those, and more, and less, and up and down and round and round
and back and forth down a rabbit hole as strange as Alice's.

Now, you send a box
of bunnies and eggs hidden beneath strips of paper that fall through
my fingers like confetti and all over the floor and everywhere,
making a mess in my silent kitchen. I pick up the gold Lindt bunny
carefully, as if he might break, but he has stayed safe and solid as the ship
that has sailed all the way across Bass Strait to bring him here, home,
where you used to be.

You Are Not / Your Poetry

I'm in love with you because you write poetry.
I'm in love with your poetry because I'm in love with you.
I'm not in love with you because you write poems for other people.
I'm not writing poems for other people because I'm in love with you.
I could never love you because you use lines you've used on me on others.
I can never love you because you use words you wrote for me for someone else
and there's always someone else.
I will always love you because you are a poet.
I will always write poetry because I love you.
I don't write poems about love.
I'm not in love with anyone.
I don't love you, I love your poetry.
I don't know the difference.

Egyptians

I tell the Egyptian guy I've just met
'I had an Egyptian boyfriend'
(boyfriend? partner? lover? fiancé?
I never knew what to call him,
and besides, the terminologies
kept changing with circumstance) –
'we were together twice – years ago –
when we were young – and again,
years later, he contacted me – and me –
being so stupid – took him back.'
'No,' says the Egyptian (*this* Egyptian –
who's known me for about five minutes)
'you're not stupid. You had hope. And
you're like me, you forgive.'
'Hmm, maybe not. He fled to Egypt,
married an Egyptian, and had a baby –
I want to kill him!' 'What's his number?'
the Egyptian says, taking out his phone
and holding it to his ear. Then I say:
'It wasn't that he couldn't commit –
he just couldn't commit to *me*.'
(It's a line I've used in one of my stories).
'Why didn't he just *tell* you?' says
the Egyptian. 'He could have just told you.'
'Well,' I say. 'Sometimes people don't know
what they want. They don't know themselves,
I mean, they don't have self-awareness.
Or they're torn. He was always caught between
two cultures. And besides, it's not so simple.'
'An Egyptian is always Egyptian,' says the Egyptian.

~

The Egyptian boyfriend shared an office
with his brother and I showed up one time
looking for the boyfriend but only the brother
was there. And I was glad. I said to him:
'Why didn't you talk to me the other night?'
'It wasn't about you,' he said. 'It's about him.'
'The first time I've ever seen you and you *snub* me?
In front of all your brother's friends? How do you
think that made me *feel*?' I said. 'It wasn't about you,'
he said. 'But I was the one on the end of it.' 'It was
a message to my brother,' he said. 'But what was it
supposed to *mean*?' I said. 'He knows what it meant.'
'And what's that?' '*Why hasn't he married you*?'
I laughed. 'You think my whole mission in life is *marriage*?'
'It's not about whether he marries you or not,' he said.
'But you just said –' 'He's never going to commit to you.'
'We're together, aren't we?' 'He is Egyptian,' he said,
as if it was an explanation (and it was). I kept to the topic
(him not talking to me in public in front of his brother's friends)
till finally he said: 'You're wasting your time with him.
You're wasting your life. I can't believe you got back with him.
I know my brother better than you do. He's never going to
commit to you. He is *Egyptian*.'

~

'His brother was right,' says the Egyptian guy. 'An Egyptian
is always Egyptian.' The Egyptian guy drives me back home,
and as I'm getting out of the car, asks if I'd like to have coffee
again some time, or maybe even dinner tomorrow night.
'Just as friends, you know,' he says. 'Nothing more.' He says

he'd never get involved with someone who's on the rebound. Let alone with me, with what I've been through. (But, oh God, haven't I heard that one before). 'Besides,' says the Egyptian guy, 'one Egyptian is more than enough.' (Actually, that's another story, but not one I'm going to tell him. At least, not now).

Haunted

I'd filled the house with furniture.

Then thought, I'd better tell the landlord
I've moved in. The house was huge;

there were empty spaces out the back,
a rambling yard. I was in Buckley St.

~

When the Egyptian left, he'd said,
Buckley St! What hope did we have?

Still I dream of my beautiful house
that was never mine.

~

I stand behind the terylene curtain
and look out the window. I watch

the neighbours. Next door, there are hippies,
former housemates of mine.

They wanted to keep bees and chickens
in the courtyard, near the compost.

A few doors down, a woman I knew
in primary school who's returned to the area.

I've never left; her face has grown hard.
People show up in your dreams to show you

something but how can you ever work out
what? My Lacanian analysis is cryptic.

~

You will live and die in Carnegie,
the last thing the Egyptian said as he left,

standing at the door, then turning towards me
from the front gate. He made it sound like some

sort of crime. Though, he was prone to
statements like that, matter-of-fact,

almost factual, as if foreseeing the future is
possible. He believed in destiny, your life

mapped out and, ultimately, chosen by God.
He knew I thought it was the life I'd chosen.

But had I? Had he? Circumstances, family
and society bearing down on us.

I threw the yellow roses he'd bought me
that Christmas Eve, my birthday, in the bin.

I asked him if he knew why and he did.

~

In the dream, I tear the terylene curtain.
Call out to the neighbours, hide behind

the torn curtain. I know they will all find out soon
that I've moved back in

without asking anyone
if I could.

Red Horse by the River

After 'Red Horse by the River,' a lithograph by Anselm van Rood

When you were a child, you drew
a red horse by a river.
Your teacher told you horses weren't red,
but black or brown or grey or white.
Your father thought your red was
too bold, too bright; a bit over-the-top
for a horse. His eyes turned cold,
I think he feared for your future.
He called you a cissy under his breath.
He blamed me for the red.
Your father never denied their existence,
though none of us had ever seen them.
We'd heard of them, out there
on the range. Someone said they'd seen
one once down there by the river, but
no one believed him. I did though,
he went into so much detail and his eyes
went all dreamy. I almost believed
I'd seen it too. Your father said
your version of red was ridiculous:
you should show only what's
real and true. I know, you said. I know.

The Object of The Father All at Sea

My little sister tells me
Tommy from kindergarten
keeps calling her
small and stupid.

Her eyes well up
and so do mine as I cry:
'So what if you're small!
And you're definitely not stupid!'

My four-year old sister looks at me
as if she's not quite sure she can trust
what her thirty-year old half-sister is saying
then is all-smiles as she changes the subject.

~

'The episode I most want to see again
is the one where Homer says:
"I'll spend time with Maggie,
the forgotten Simpson,"' my sister says.

'Forgotten?' I say. I've never seen *The Simpsons*
so my sister (who's now seven) explains:
Maggie's a baby; she can't talk; she's not noticed,
though she's *sooo* cute. What happens is –

Homer enters Maggie's room and pokes her awake
and says: "I'm going to spend time with you!"
Maggie looks up from half-sleep
to a stranger with a strange face

just out of dreamland, this face in her face
is a disoriented and misshapen head
seen through half-open eyes
and a world that's weird where

a father seems suddenly unfamiliar.
Homer and Maggie take off in the car
driving by the beach.
Maggie points out a butterfly out the window

but Homer (who never listens to anybody)
says: "That's a good idea, Maggie."
She points again but he doesn't see
or understand what she means.

Instead, he takes her to the sea where he believes
she wants to be because that's where
he wants to be. "Under the sea
is the solution for everything," he says.

Maggie stays safely on the shore.
Scared of the water and now
slightly scared of the mask her father
is wearing; what it does to his face.

A green sea-monster,
blowing bubbles as he goes under.
She watches as he's suddenly caught in a rip,
spluttering and floundering like a fish

out of water. She moves
towards the sea slowly
puts one toe in, tentative,
then marches straight out

to save him. Grabbing hold of him with one arm
and swimming with the other
until they reach the shore
where the whole family is waiting.

Her mother, Marge, cries: "How did you do it?
How could you do that —
when you're so *small?*"
'I love that line,' my little sister says.

Lessons on Life from My Sister in First Year

After 'Why Be Happy When You Could Be Normal' by Jeanette Winterson

I just want to enjoy things I don't want to think about them. don't you do anything for fun you can't help yourself, you have to deconstruct everything. you have to talk about the ultimate meaning of everything you can't just watch something and enjoy it. ok yes there's *The Sound of Music* I'll grant you that. yes you love it but I'll bet. see there you go. you don't love it just for the music and the story. you have to analyse it and deconstruct it through some particular perspective and now it's feminism of course. I just want to enjoy the fucking movie I don't care if Maria's some feminist heroine (or hero) refusing and resisting oppression and how she has her own autonomy that won't be squashed by man or nun or even God Herself. why do you do that? can't you just take anything on face value? what do you do sit there in the theatre tearing it apart ripping it to shreds till there's nothing left. can't you just. shit. it's not that. I'm not against thinking. I just don't want to do it all the time. I don't want to think or talk about the meaning of everything. I don't see why you have to deconstruct everything and not just take it more lightly or something. you take it all so seriously. if you think about what it all means you're going to end up being critical. you're going to end up liking nothing. you're not going to enjoy anything. that's what happens if you try to work out things and the meaning in everything. and it will get in the way of having a good time. you'll drive yourself crazy thinking about what it all means and everyone else. otherwise you're just going to make yourself unhappy. all of us. love you. hey. you know helping me with my essays I couldn't have done it without you. yeah well meaning really mattered then. but that's what you have to do at uni. it doesn't mean you have to do it all the time and everywhere with everything. dad says you think too much. mum thinks you're full of shit. sometimes. I just think people who don't think too much are happier. that's what life's about right? I mean thinking like that. you'd be happier if you didn't think so much don't you think? does it make you happy? yeah well what was that thing you told me about? some title or book or something? oh yeah. *Why Be Happy When You Could Be Normal?* exactly. I mean like really. you'd just be happier if you could be normal. don't you think?

Girl in Front

Girl right in front of me asks: 'Do you know how to spell "Madame?"'
'Give it a go,' I say.
Girl in front bows her head, writes nothing, looks up and stares
out the window, looks across at me and catches my eye, says:
'Do you know French?'
'No.'
'Oh.'
Girl at the front dips her head down, writes a word, looks up, says:
'Do you know how to spell "evening"?'
'You try it,' I say in a very kind tone.
Girl in front sighs, moans, clicks her pen, chews it, and all the while
keeps looking at me till she whispers, 'Have you got any liquid paper because
I've kind of made a mistake.'
The only thing written on her paper is her name.
'Girls,' I say to all of them. 'It's okay to make mistakes. Don't leave any blanks.
Guessing is good. Just try. That's what we're here for: to learn. It doesn't matter
if you get things wrong. That's how we learn. From our mistakes.'
Girl at the front scribbles a minute, then is out of her seat and sidles up
beside me, says: 'I don't understand this.'
I explain the instructions to her, as I've been instructed to do
from the lesson plan left for the emergency teacher.
And as I already have. At the outset.
'Oh,' she says. 'Now I get it.'
'Good.'
Girl goes back to the front, bows her head, looks up, says:
'Do you know the answer to Number 2?'
'No I don't. This is a test.'
'Yeah I know. But the thing is, I don't have any answers.'
It's my first year out – neither do I.

In the best of all possible worlds

I am sick. He calls every day.
He says – *In the best of all possible worlds,*
I'd be bringing you orange juice.
I cry. After he hangs up I am alone
in the small place I've moved to.
I hear the family next door talking at
night. The walls here are thin.
I have the television on, in the background.
I heat up a meal my mother made me.
In the best of all possible worlds,
you would be here. But you're not.
So here I am, alone and ailing.
I don't think I'll ever recover.

Morsels

For Brenda Palmer

Here are the crumbs you left me,
fallen on floorboards in a line
that leads to the closed front door.
Here is the softness that's come
over me, the swollen tenderness
bruising at the slightest touch.
There are the cards you hold
in your hand, cryptic. A friend
wrote to me using the word
quicksand and I reeled from it.
I tear at cuticles, the edges of
skin bleed. The friend said *still,*
you keep bobbing up to the surface,
you're still swimming. And that's true,
but who wants the love of their life –
their *life* – summed up as quicksand?
I head out the front door. I leave
a trail so you can find me.

Your Mind on the Dead

My father goes to more funerals than anyone I've ever known.
It's not because of his age, or that he knows so many people
(though he does know a lot of people). Even an ex-boyfriend
of mine that my father never liked (and my father likes everyone,
though scratch beneath the surface and he's actually quite critical,
and judgemental – he just doesn't come across that way because
he hides it, you never know what he's really thinking behind his
glasses and in fact, I often only find out when he's confronted or
feeling cornered and then he comes out with things I almost wish
I hadn't heard, for their lack of empathy and understanding, which
can be staggering) – he went to that funeral of the ex he didn't like
(and I didn't).

The last time I saw my father I told him I'd written
a poem about him called *Your Mind on the Dead (While the Living
Are Still With You)*. He took a while to take it in then I saw it register
on his face and shortly after that he fled (though that's not unusual).
Always in a rush, always has to go. Always saying *I've got places
to go and promises to keep.* Even when he's there, he's not really there.
I've been asking (a few weeks now) – telling my father I want to talk
to him about my brother. He still hasn't made a time. Something always
comes up or he simply never manages to get back to me. My mother
said to me *Why don't you say to him – I'm asking you for ONE hour
out of your life – do you think you could spare that?* And she said
sometimes she says to him *You wouldn't want to have REGRETS,
would you?* I looked at my mother in surprise. She really has learnt
something from life. She sees herself as stupid. Uneducated. Illiterate.
And yet, she can often find better words than I can; comes out with
things where you think, Jesus, where did that come from? I couldn't
believe she had those words at her fingertips when I couldn't think

of a single thing to say to my father about the fact that I'd told him
I need to talk to him about his son and I haven't heard back from him.
He knows it's serious. But still. Still haven't heard from him. Or the fact
that he can go to the funerals of people who are practically strangers
but he can't spend an hour with his daughter to talk about his son.

My ex-partner used to say one day he's going to write a story called
The Man Who Went to Funerals if I don't do it first. I keep trying
to work it out − why my father does it − what does it all mean −
what's his motive. I asked the ex-partner (a psychologist) − I took it
to my therapist (a psychotherapist/analyst) − but I still don't know why
my father has this thing about funerals and I don't know what it will take
to ever find out.

Writing Companion

Companion, from the Latin: 'sharer of bread': for Alicia Sometimes

She asked if
we should swap
words but I'd already
grown attached.
How quick
the hand holds on
to *gunmetal* and *red*,
how soon
the heart says pretty
and opens then
clasps. The taste of
sounds on the tongue,
the sharp tang
of consonants,
how the vowels curl.
I hand them over,
reluctant, then,
the moments of
suspension, hovering
in empty space,
and finally, the return,
where all the words rush
and anything is possible.

Laura's Pergolas

After 'Persian Pergolas,' Installation, blown and sheet glass, by Dale Chihuly

We stumble through, our throats
thrown back, our eyes raised and our necks
twisted, our heads lolling around
as if separate from the rest of us;
our fingers reach out, the tips floating
like seaweed and as we are looking up,
we are almost falling over legs and arms;
our eyes wear a glazed look
as if we're not quite used to seeing,
like spacemen discovering a new planet,
all the strange and exotic specimens,
possibly even new and alien species,
of which we may or may not be a part; and then
we lie on the floor in the National Gallery,
not just you and I but all of us, like lovers,
bodies strewn in a corridor
bathed in eerie yellow light like
morning on the moon. Through the glass ceiling
strange glass shapes – coral, pergolas,
shells, and oysters – suspend themselves
in air that seems to shine with crystal;
colours more surreal than colour
and shapes so weird and wonderful
they might be slightly scary, sea-creatures
at the bottom of the ocean, separated from us
by glass yet immersing us in waves
washing over us as we join the others
on the ocean floor.

~

Later I send my little sister, Laura,
a postcard of the Dale Chihuly ceiling
at the National Gallery in Canberra:
this reminds me of you swimming through
the New Year every summer, I write.

I take you with me on every trip like a charm
or rosary. I offer up small prayers to a God
who will protect you. I write to you from
everywhere, and often, but we don't mention it
until the drawing you've done this day –
from memory! – at your first best friend's house.
You bring this with you to give it to me as a gift,
holding it out towards me as if you know
how much it will mean to me.

Your picture is an abstract painting in progress
where colours and shapes move and breathe and
sprawl around the page in their own good time:
your swirls of texta and coloured pencils and crayons
of round full shapes, of dinosaurs and flowers and birds,
wild with fat fingers; a young girl stretching her arms
for flight. I place your picture alongside my postcard
to remember where one begins and another takes off
and how they come together.

'It's not meant for a wall,' you tell me with all the authority
of a seven-year old when you see it. You want the sun to
shine through my window, through your dinosaurs and flowers
and birds, like the light filtering through shapes in the glass ceiling.
But I know it would fade over time and I want it to keep it,

want it to last forever. 'I wonder if we'll be close when you grow up,' I say suddenly. You sound so small when you say in an anxious voice, your little face concerned: 'I hope we stay just the same as we are now.'

The Bride Who Became Frightened
When She Saw Life Opened

The Bride Who Became Frightened When She Saw Life Opened

After 'The Bride Frightened At Seeing Life Opened,' a painting by Frida Kahlo

She hasn't read a book in seven years
he doesn't like the light on
if she gets in before him   he says nothing
she could read all night
but the thing is   he's in bed by nine
every night   every night she has
something to do   she folds their washing
in three piles on the kitchen bench and once
he's passing through   and it's on his way
so   she asks him to take one pile
the kids' clothes   put them on the bed
that's all she asks   he wouldn't have to open
a cupboard or a drawer
but he refuses   another time
she's peeling potatoes and stacking dishes
and showing Sonya how to tie a shoelace
in a double knot   she asks him to take the rubbish
out   but he says no   why should he?
she's closer to the door and she says
for the first time ever   about anybody
I hate you   to the window
as if she's talking to herself   or talking
about the weather and she goes back
to peeling the potatoes.

The Call

I called my mother last night from the city
while I waited for the train.
I began with *how did you go today?*
but really, I was calling for the name
of a hairdresser.

Anyway, it was just
a check-up. My brother driving her
to the Alfred. Lung cancer long behind her.
Her poor arthritic leg. An x-ray.

Her voice was full of stones.
I heard the dampness beneath her breath.
The stones stopped me. She said
she'd tell me later, tomorrow.

She'd sat up straight after surgery
as if nothing had happened.
I'm still here, she said.

Now I'm thinking of all the weekends
I didn't take her with me to Warburton or to sit
in the sun somewhere. Picnics, Italy.
Byron Bay.

I called my mother last night
and she said she'd call me first thing
in the morning with the name and number
of the hairdresser. That was all.

Stones in my throat, as I
hung up the phone and watched the brilliant lights
of the train hurtling closer and closer.

Annotated Memories

I.

Then there's the letters I find amongst your photos in boxes
underneath our bed, letters filled with longing, for your body,
your kisses; the soft sweet smell of you. She sounds
ludicrously young: *how I long to lie with you*
again in the sunroom and stroke your hair and your face
how I long to be together again and how much you've
taught me — a large loose scrawl like a schoolgirl.
And here you are on a lawn in the seventies with the girl
of the letters who has long brown hair and is sitting beside you
smiling. Your hair is long too, waving in the wind.
Captured on camera smack in the middle of a marriage
that lasted three years. And this is not your wife but
a girl whose name is unknown to me.

I see scrawled at the end of one of her letters an annotation
in your hand: 'The formality of the expression is due to
the restrictions of our respective partners.'
Yep, sure sounds like you.

It's a long time since we exchanged stories, told each other our histories.
Yours was full of women who'd done you wrong. Women had always
treated you badly; been unfaithful. I'd swear you had tears in your eyes
just thinking of them. I believed your stories, I had no reason not to.

II.
I ask you *who's this?*
And you tell me her name.
And I say *you've never mentioned her before.*
And you say *she wasn't important.*
And I say *she sounded pretty keen.*
And you shrug and say *I wasn't crazy about her.*
And then I ask *and what about this last line of the love letter –*
in your hand – like an annotation – what does it mean?
It means what it means you say
as if it's perfectly clear
and I suppose it is.

III.
And then I come across, in one of your boxes, a (first) marriage
to a woman whose name you've mentioned, but never the marriage.
Not the marriage I know about. The one with the mother of your child.

All I'm trying to do is make a collage for your fiftieth
but clearly your history is something that can never be framed.
I put the (first) wedding photo away, back into the box under our bed,
where you seem to think it belongs.

IV.
I keep the brown-haired girl of the love letters; include her in the collage.
But at night I lie there thinking of everything I've culled
in making this collage. I'm writing a speech too but it's
getting harder and harder to know what to say.

The Photograph Travels With Us Through Time

1.

You tape us, carefully, on the cover of your diary
like a premonition. This is our year. A grainy shot,
we are a splash of light and darkness, my tanned shoulders
rising from my slinky black dress, your skin and hair
so white in contrast. Your big black book is personal,
reveals your life for you in colour. Our faces whiz past
as you map out each working week. There we are
as we were then. Before. And me there as a reminder
your every working day.

That same year we end up torn up and thrown away,
our smiling faces young, milk spilt all over us.
The crumbs smudge our eyes. You show us all
how angry you are – you show her it's over,
you show me. I find myself in the rubbish at home.
Your black work diary is shiny where the cellotape
left its mark. You're the one carrying on as if
you're the one who's been betrayed.

The same shot sits in a silver frame on your desk –
that will disappear too. I wonder when you take it away,
at which point, what moment seemed the right one.
Was it not long after I left or when I returned?
Me there as a reminder your every working day.

ll.
We surface in the silver frame in your new workplace.
This is a new year. We sit beside your daughter as a baby.
My long black hair leans towards you with a life of its own.
That was before I went short. Before you shaved.
Before. I don't recognize the beardless face
you bring to the airport.

You advertise us through your window,
we are turned towards people who pass us by,
registering the instant, and moving on.
I don't say it is without meaning.
We are objects, pieces of furniture:
you don't really need to look at us.
It is enough that we exist, proof.

That same year you and I end up tossed in a drawer.
Why would I be there, captured, continuing,
when you've told everyone at work
I'm leaving you. I wonder if you'll put it back
now I've stayed. I always look for it when I'm there
as if it will tell me where we are.

lll.
I have the same photo still on my desk, never moved.
I imagine her sailing into our flat, a stranger, seeing my study,
taking in the photo. Or did you hide it away out of sight?
And would we call that a whim or an act of will?
No, you'd leave it there, wouldn't you.

The Day You Left

There were dreams last night
        and you were not in them.

I watched your ship as it moved so slowly.

And stood on the shore
        as if I was safe.

The moon became only a mention, a speck.

The ocean was dark
        and so still.

There was nothing there, just this
        blank silence.

The night was not warm.

I pulled my coat tighter.

Thought about going home,
        the key in the lock.

Putting the heater on.

Saw the house in my head
        as it waited for me.

Our singing group would be half-over
        by the time I got there.

If I went.

And then, the absence
        of the ship.

I stared at the space
        where the ship had been.

And I thought
        now I understand.

Negative capability
        finally made sense to me.

But it felt too late.

Your poetry went with you
        and I don't mean your books.

I arrived just before tea-break.

I remember them surrounding me,
        like a circle, as I stumbled in
        telling them
                      he's gone.

I really believed that night
        singing would save me.

But what I remember is
        all the faces turning to see me
        when I stood at the door

hesitating, the deep breath I took
before I launched into

the outstretched arms,

the bright warm hum
of the room.

Not Sending You Poetry

I.

Your books on my glass coffee table –
  Reflections of a Temporary Self –
    This Is What Gives Us Time –
new books by poets you used to know in your youth   your Brunswick days
      with Jane and Margo and all the others   you loved and lost
                    and wrote poems for.

You have urged me out of the dark
        to the launches of books of poetry
          into the world.

You want signatures   you want me to think of something beyond myself
        and poetry and poets might do it.

                This was always your promise.

You want me to send   the books across Bass Strait   where you are now
        living the life time has given you   while I wait here hoping this
              is a temporary self.

The books in a certain light cast shadows   on the glass.
      Their covers call across the room
            look, look at me and remember –
                this night   that self   what time gives us.

If I send them now   there'll be a clear outline
          that says here was something and now
                    empty spaces rimmed by dust
                              the shapes of something
                                        taken away or gone.

II.

I withhold what you want from me   like a punishment.
       Such a simple thing   to go to the Post Office   send off a parcel.
            I'm struggling with the simplest things.
                    You were supposed to come back.
                        This was our glass   our books on the table.

One of the poets writes about marriage.
                Longevity, love.
                    Still together after all this time.

It's almost unbearable   I want to say to you –
              you will never have books like this there.

                  You will never have there what you can have here.

And what am I now – your connection to the mainland?
            Your own private postal service   for all the poetry
                and all the world you can't access   on the island?

In Tasmania   they say they're going to Australia
            when they mean Melbourne.

You call it *Deliverance with cars*   it's a good line   you're good with lines.

But this line's growing fainter. Soon I won't be able to hear you
　　　standing beside me. Soon I won't be looking over my shoulder
　　　　　making sure　　　　　you're still there.

I didn't expect life to turn out like this　　　I say.
　　　It's still turning　　　you say.

Daddy Long Legs

It started with one. In the corner behind the tv.

Then there was another. Near the front door. Then there were
two, in my bedroom. They coveted corners, ceilings, or edges
of things. *There must be a nest,* said my mother, as if she was
an expert. She suggested vacuuming, *but you'd have to make sure,*

she said, *cover the vacuum so they can't get out.* I knew
she could imagine me, taking the hose, heaving the thing out.
Dropping it, screaming; breaking it, as all those legs walked out.
Are they inviting their friends? Is it something about this house?

It never dawns on me to dust. I want to know their mystery.

I leave them there, as proof. Of what, I can't say. I want to get rid of them.
It's not as if this house is haunted. Who am I kidding? Of course it is.
You are not here. You never noticed cobwebs anyway, you allowed
them to accumulate. You always kept things clean on the surface.

So I leave the spiders there. It doesn't matter how harmless they are,
I'm still scared of them. I'm frightened of killing them, I fear they
might call all their friends. Four or five – at a stretch six– I can contain.
But if they keep coming, I don't know what I'll do.

I know one thing though: there's no point calling you.

Layers

I.

I haven't heard from you in four days   I refuse to wear layers

  I've lived here all my life but never grown used to this climate

I resist   refuse to compromise   you have grown cold

   I don't know if you are still coming back

I try to be patient   not gallop towards you   beg or plead

    You lurk beneath everything

The threat of cutting off   if I say or do anything you don't like

   There are things said which should be unutterable

II.

It's not in the words   it's always the weight of them

   The weight of words in our hands like water

You stole those words from me I said you were welcome to them

   now I'm not so sure

Januaries

I remember once when Januaries were wild. When I went to Egypt. When I sat
in a counsellor's room and said – *what am I going to do with my life?*

And the counsellor said – *you've been here before*. And reminded me I often
see him in January. I remember when beginnings, when friendships were easy.

Life so casual. Before I realized Leonard Cohen would die. I'd thought
I'd take my brother next time but there was no next. I read countless books

on death and dying yet still never realize we're all going to die. How is it
possible my father is turning seventy-seven in six days? The uncle I loved most

gone. And the last time I saw you. There were stains all over your sweatshirt.
You stumbled along the street. Tiny hills were too hard. There were pieces

of shit on your toilet seat. And a house where every corner was filled
with dust. Your house was steeped in it. I suddenly saw you were

an emergency. I wanted to lift you out of your urgent situation and bring you
back. To life, to Melbourne, to me. Money is not easy and has all our lives

stopped us. We live in a rich poverty. I remember once when Decembers
were times we were together, the two of us, celebrating Christmas, as if

we made a family, the only one that would have us, the only one we could
be with. We come together, we come apart. Here is my heart. You don't

deserve it. Sometimes we don't know what we're letting ourselves in for
until that moment we see it.

Horses

Suddenly a black cow outside a fence.
A strange strangled sound everywhere.
All the cows calling. I stop singing.
An ancient knowing in its old eyes.
I see how it watches as I move past.
Careful and slow. Leave it standing there.
Forgotten till dinner when I tell Joseph.
He pushes peas and gravy aside.
Rushes out in the black night searching.
It's not one of ours. But they're bloody expensive,
you know. I don't know. The closest I come is roast.
I am a city girl frightened of a cow outside a fence.
I see the streets of Spain where the bulls ran.
Butting backpackers. An Australian
or two. The bulls gone mad and let loose.
Creatures are capable of anything.

Then the next day along that same road.
Up ahead four horses trotting along then grazing.
And slow then quick shadows that seem like people.
Surely that's a small frame. A girl in jodphurs. A cap.
Tiny beside the horses. I keep to the side of the road.
The chestnut veers towards me as if it might nuzzle.
And say hello or never stop but go right through me.
And I hold my breath. Keep walking the way you do.
With dogs. Never show fear. I'm not sure about horses.
But it turns in another direction just before it nears.
It turns away from me heading straight ahead.
So that the others look up and canter to catch up
with this one who has somewhere to go.

Two women in a ute at a snail pace.
With a window down slow as they near.
Are you looking for horses?
One has wild hair. Exhausted eyes. A hard face.
Up too early or too long. And now I speak
like a local with my knowledge of territory.
They're up McNamara's Road – the next road
to the left. It's as if she's never heard of it.
Can't quite work out what I mean. Her lost face.
I point. She nods. And they're gone. And now
I wish I took that extra moment to ask
where they'd come from. Those horses.
Heading down the road so far from home.
And where they're going.

Embodiment in Quill

For Gay Lynch

I have been rearranging my ankles.

They no longer sit at the end of my legs,
			they are only a suggestion.
						I feel loose, and lighter.

I have been chanting too, my voice is fine
				but I no longer want words,
						just sounds.

My hair has grown long but I'm
				keeping it high on my head.
						I seem taller.

Meanwhile, my clothes grow small and smell.
				I ignore them. And housekeeping is
						not for women who write.

Neither is maintenance. I've thrown out all my stilettos,
				I don't know how to wear stockings.
						Once, I lay on my bed,

contorted, for a pair of fishnets. I never forgot
				how painful it was. It wasn't physical.
						That I could bear.

A living being is making his way through the house.
				I shut out dishes in the kitchen,
						and keep my door open.

After 'Still Life with Babette's Jug #2'

Acrylic on paper, by Anselm van Rood

You take a white jug and you see shadows, blues and greys hover
like halos, like surfaces, like ghosts at the edge of boundaries,
a thin curving handle like an ear you can see through,
shapes and triangles of roses and cerulean blue and then black,
and then the ear becomes an inverted tear, or a cartoon balloon
for someone to speak, and now the body of the jug's smudges
take on qualities of the moon while the rim fills with aqua blue
to swim in, and yet that centering of white is not where you begin
for it's obvious it's oranges in their bright bold orbs that verge on
the lusciousness of peaches in a brown bowl, and how brown is not
after all boring but the comfort of wood and blocks and warm
and a sprig of green sits in a corner like a talisman, like a surprise
of spring and the light-as-a-touch feather amongst solid things,
and you place three pears on a soft-yellow plate, round blobs
of bright green, and yellow-greens merging into each other, and
then the one that is orange on one side and greenyellow on the
other, as if someone has come and spliced it in half with a colour
wand, it sits there not divided but whole in its two coloured selves,
and they sit together like siblings, like matryoshka dolls, waiting
and the bare suggestion of silver blade and black handle of a knife
lying across the plate like something that might be used but could
be left, and you take a tall orange bottle but this isn't the orange
of oranges, this is deeper and darker, something that suggests and
almost seeps into the splash of red beside it, and then you have two
pink blocks, like books, one on top of the other, or breadboards,
this light lovely pink that's soft and strange, you don't often see
this shade that shines like a light on water in a pink sun, but pale,
but not pallid, but bright, and there you place a golden bottle,
as if you have taken the yellow-orange blaze of the sun and

burnished it, brought it here to warm the soft pinkness of slabs,
shapes that are round and voluptuous on top of squares and
surrounded by rectangles and triangles and edges of things,
there is no beginning here, not oranges, not a bright white jug,
possibly it's a table, you start with what's solid then move to
what you put onto it, this table that is verdant green grass,
something for every orange and yellow and gold and pink to
sit down, as if stable, as if called upon and summoned, but only
perhaps for this moment, and then you notice even the gold
has a tiny triangle, like a tease, a taste of pink, like a flickering
page, a suggestion, as if the solid pinkness of slabs have leapt
out of their boxes, a butterfly's wings leaving its imprint
on gold, and then there are other shapes that suggest tables,
dimensions, depth, this cobalt blue so bright, so shimmering,
and then the bottle with its limbs and its shoulders standing
there, almost the same colour, and yet not, its lines both
blurred and clear and surrounded, right next to olive green,
two bottle-shapes, their bodies lightly touching, and close,
like lovers, and tall and slim, in the background, but sure,
and then more squares and more cobalt blue and tables almost
on top of tables, as in some higher, some lower, and all together,
and the suddenness of two black bowls of small oranges, one
large and high, almost a bucket, a gigantic cup, and the other
smaller, rounder, and only one with a half-sun of lemon,
and inside both bowls that luminous white, that smooth shiny
suggestion again, and on a bright white square sits a green-lemon
something, a perfect circle with softly blurred edges, a serviette
or placemat seems too ordinary to sit on this table and yet everything
that's ordinary and extraordinary is simultaneously suggested, as
you take all these shapes and colours and place them seemingly
randomly alongside and amongst each other, and we don't know
where to begin, except everywhere, and you have given us everything.

The Memory of Colour

After your painting 'Angophora, Salamander Bay 2001' by David Rose
I.M. Judith Rodriguez

I have decided to remain vertical.
Though there are footprints all over
my eyelids, my body,
I haul myself out of bed and

into bathers, knowing
how a day begins can keep you
upright just a little bit longer.
These morning routines,

like cats, wait on the window sill.
I am no longer a woman who wears
a hat and rides her bike around
Carnegie but now and then I return to

my bike like a long-lost friend.
I slip out of my sandals and leave them
on concrete while I walk in
bare feet all the way to the place

where I lock the bike.
The walk back is about twenty steps
and sometimes that is all it takes
to remember green, to feel it

in your feet. To feel practically feline.
I hover on the first step then wade right in.
I hold the colour of the sky
in my arms, and swim.

Acknowledgements

Poems in this collection have been previously published in *Australian Poetry Anthology, Australian Poetry Journal, Westerly, Overland, Red Room Poetry, SETU (U.S./India), Live Encounters (U.S.), Eureka Street, Not Very Quiet, The Victorian Writer, Marrickville Pause, The Blue Nib (Ireland), Solace: ACU Poetry Prize Anthology, The Sky Falls Down: Anthology of Loss, Verity La, Shots from the Chamber: An Anthology of poems by the Chamber Poets, Uneven Floor, foam: e,* and *Muse;* and awarded/ finalist/ highly commended /commended for the following prizes: 2021: Newcastle Poetry Prize (Second Prize), Woorilla Poetry Prize, My Brother Jack Poetry Award, Ada Cambridge Poetry Award, Yeats Poetry Prize. 2020: My Brother Jack Poetry Awards (First Prize), Woorilla Poetry Prize, Bruce Dawe Poetry Prize. 2017 – 2018: Melbourne Poets Union International Poetry Prize, My Brother Jack Poetry Award, Adrien Abbott Poetry Prize (2015 – 2018).

The poem 'Not Sending You Poetry' refers to the following books of poetry: *This Is What Gives Us Time* (Gloria SMH Press, 2016) by Kevin Brophy; and *Reflections of a Temporary Self* (Collective Effort Press, 2015) by Grant Caldwell.

This book was mostly written and completed on the lands of the Boonwurrung people. I want to express my gratitude to the traditional owners and custodians of this land, Elders past, present and emerging. Some of these poems were also conceived/written during my Poetry Residency at the Banff Arts Centre, Canada. I express my gratitude to traditional owners and to the Banff Centre.

I would like to firstly thank Puncher and Wattmann, whom I'm thrilled to be published by. Huge thank you to David Musgrave. To Morgan Arnett. And to Ross Gillett, for sensitive, incisive editing. Enormous respect and gratitude for the work you all do.

I would like also to thank the editors of journals and anthologies in which my poems in this collection were published; the organisers of awards/prizes who support poets and poetry; and Poetry Reading convenors who have invited me to read. All so important to the evolution of this book and to my work finding a home here.

I worked on this manuscript most significantly during this pandemic. I would like to thank family and friends in my life who made such a difference. Working on this book helped sustain me through very challenging times. Equally important to my work are the people in my life. I would not have been able to do this work without you.

Heartfelt gratitude for invaluable feedback from Katia Ariel and Ann Shenfield; and to Kevin Brophy, Anne Elvey and Jennifer Compton, for their endorsements for this book cover and ongoing support. And also, thank you to Katia Ariel, Ann Shenfield, Emilie Collyer, Ann Locanini, Alex Skovron, and Marcia Jacobs, for endorsements and all your support.

Huge and heartfelt thank you to Marion May Campbell and Kathleen Mary Fallon, for reading my work and for extraordinary generosity.

Thank you also for feedback on poems and support: Anne M. Carson, Jennifer Compton, Rose Lucas, Belinda Rule, Alice Allan, Michelle Leber, Coral Carter, Gabrielle Everall, Claire Gaskin, and Helen Jarvis.

Thank you to writing companions, Tim Clark, Cindy Sullivan, Helen Jarvis and Margie Ulbrick; and to Elzbieta Zorska, Janine Gollant, Demi Liapis, Gay Lynch, and Lisa McNiece. For support and friendship, thank you all. And to Merinda Strahan, heartfelt thanks.

To Richard Lawton, Miche Lewin and the Soulsong Singing Group community, and Chris Mitchison, thank you. And also to Catherine Mundy, Camille Nurka, Malcolm Connell, Alicia Sometimes, and Cath Drake.

A huge thank you to Anselm van Rood for the detail from his beautiful painting 'St Kilda Morning: Souvenir of Luxor' on the cover of this book; and to Libby Austen for the wonderful cover design, and much more.

And a very special thank you and indebtedness to Lyndon Walker, for the ongoing literary and life conversation and supportive friendship. Much love and thanks.

And to my family, much love and much gratitude, for being there for me in meaningful ways.

About the Author

Gayelene Carbis is an Australian/Chinese/Irish/Cornish writer who lives and works on the unceded land of the Boonwurrung people.

Her first book of poetry, *Anecdotal Evidence* (Five Islands Press) was awarded Finalist, International Book Awards, 2019 (U.S.). In 2021, she was awarded Second Prize, Newcastle Poetry Prize; and Highly Commended/Commended in the Woorilla, My Brother Jack, Ada Cambridge, and Yeats Poetry Awards. In 2020, she won First Prize, My Brother Jack Poetry Award; was Highly Commended in the Woorilla Poetry Prize; and Finalist in the Bruce Dawe Poetry Prize.

In prose, Gayelene recently won Second Prize, My Brother Jack Short Story Award; and her work has been Shortlisted/Finalist for various prizes, including *The Age*/Readings and *ABR* Elizabeth Jolley Short Story Prizes; Lord Mayor's Creative Writing Award; Fish Short Story and Memoir Prizes (Ireland); and Best Small Fictions. Her short stories and creative non-fiction have been published widely in journals/anthologies, in Australia and overseas.

Gayelene has read her poetry in Australia and internationally, including in New York, Canada, Italy, Greece, and Egypt. She was awarded a Scholarship Poetry Residency at the Banff Centre, Canada (2012). Gayelene has also written over twenty plays and one-woman shows, staged in Australia and internationally.

Gayelene teaches Creative Writing in universities/creative writing programs; is Poet-in-Residence in schools; and works as a creative writing mentor/manuscript assessor. She was nominated for a Teaching Excellence Award (Australian College of Applied Psychology, 2010). She is currently teaching English for Academic Purposes at ACU and Poetry at The Avenue.

Gayelene was Finalist in the Nilumbik Prize for Contemporary Writing (Poetry) 2022 and is currently nominated for the Ros Spencer Poetry Prize. She has recently completed her first collection of short stories/creative non-fiction.